SPILLIN DA PHIYAH:

EDITED VERSIONS

OF MY SOUL

JAYNE PHLOW

SPILLIN DA PHIYAH: EDITED VERSIONS OF MY SOUL

Printed in the United States of America

ISBN-13:978-0692586921
ISBN-10:069258692X

Printed by Createspace 2015
Published by BlaqRayn Publishing Plus 2015

BIO

TIFFANY D. GLOVER, AKA JAYNE PHLOW, IS A 3-TIMES PUBLISHED AUTHOR, AS WELL AS A POET; SPOKEN WORD ARTIST; BLOGTALK RADIO HOST; EDITOR; AND SINGLE MOTHER TO HER 16-YEAR OLD SON, T'ZHEAN.

SHE IS A GRADUATE OF SPRINGFIELD COLLEGE'S SCHOOL OF HUMAN SERVICES, WHERE SHE OBTAINED HER MASTER'S DEGREE IN COMMUNITY COUNSELING PSYCHOLOGY AND IS CURRENTLY

ATTENDING WEBSTER UNIVERSITY IN PURSUIT OF HER LICENSED PROFESSIONAL COUNSELOR (LPC) CERTIFICATION. SHE HOPES TO USE HER DEGREE, COMBINED WITH HER LOVE OF POETRY, SPOKEN WORD AND TRAVEL, TO EMPOWER WOMEN, YOUNG AND NOT SO YOUNG, WHO ARE BATTLING SELF-ESTEEM ISSUES TO TRANSITION THEMSELVES FROM EMOTIONALLY DEBILITATING RELATIONSHIPS.

SPILLIN DA PHIYAH

THANK YOU

THANK YOU ALL FOR ALL OF THE
LOVE, ENCOURAGEMENT, SUPPORT AND
OPPORTUNITIES
THAT YOU HAVE BLESSED ME WITH AND CONTINUE TO
BLESS ME WITH.
YOU HAVE NO IDEA HOW MUCH I APPRECIATE
YOU.

~I AM JAYNE PHLOW~

EDITED VERSIONS OF MY SOUL

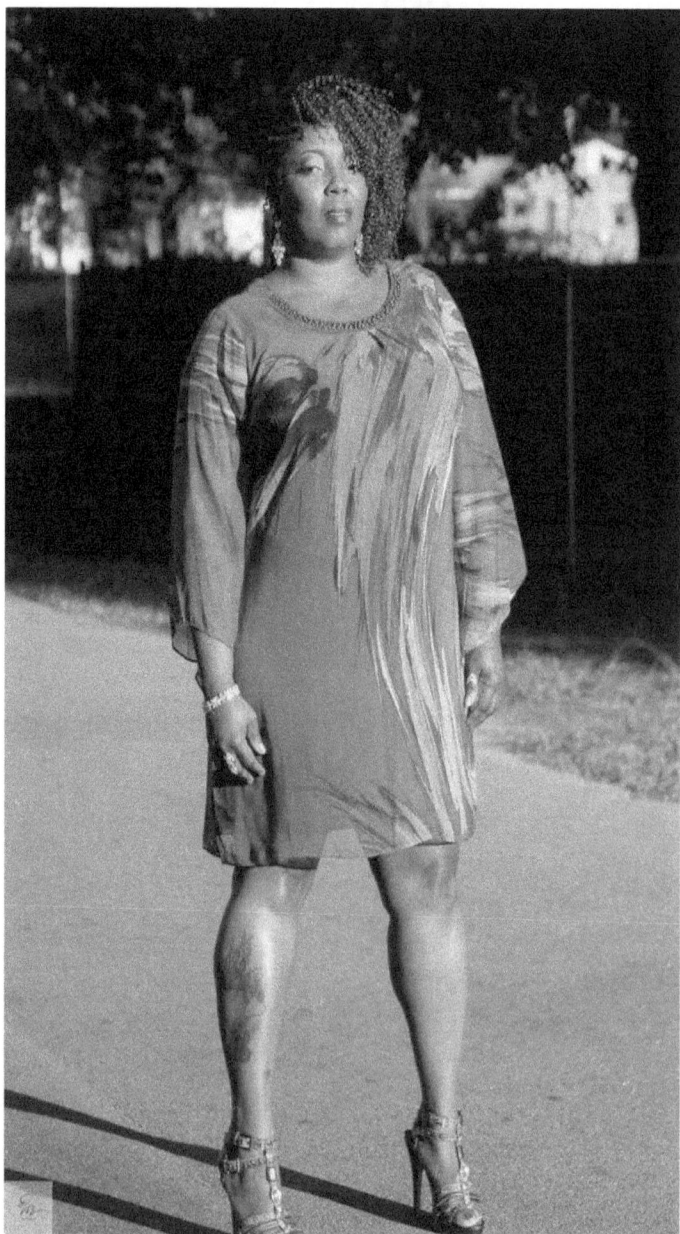

HE LOVES ME...

EDITED VERSIONS OF MY SOUL

AND STILL WE DANCE

After all these years, you still make feel as young as
the day we first met
You don't see my hair filled with grey
Nor do you see my varicose veins
You still smile at the way my hips sway

Despite my few aches and pains you continue to
woo me
Bringing me flowers and such
Your fingers still send electric shocks through me
At even the slightest touch

Your silly jokes still make me chuckle
And your kisses still make me melt
The love we make still makes my knees buckle
I've remained the one and only notch in your belt

Our impromptu living room dances
As Billie and Nat croon behind us
Still sends me swingin' as we steal little glances
Losing ourselves in a world where no one can find
us

After all these years, you still call me your "girl"
And I still call you "my guy"
40 years of this dip, this spin, this twirl
You keep me floating on air...I believe I can fly

We're in this thing "til death do we part"
So please God, grant us both long life
So that we may live each day as a brand new start

SPILLIN DA PHIYAH

On our journey as husband and wife

February 21, 2015

EDITED VERSIONS OF MY SOUL

ANTICIPATION

I'm SOOOOOOO ready to feel love
Love sent and blessed by the Heavens above

Love Absolutely
Love Beautifully
Love Courageously
Love Divinely
Love Exceptionally
Love Fervently
Love Gloriously
Love Harmoniously
Love Incredibly
Love Justifiably
Love Kindredly
Love Liberatingly
Love Marvelously
Love Nobly
Love Outstandingly
Love Perfectly
Love Quintessentially
Love Respectfully
Love Supremely
Love Tantilizingly
Love Ubiquitously
Love Vivaciously
Love Wondrously
Love Xcellently
Love Yearningly
Love Zealously
Love

Love that rains down from the Heavens above

SPILLIN DA PHIYAH

Lord please bless me with THAT kind of
LOVE…..of myself

January 3, 2014

EDITED VERSIONS OF MY SOUL

HE IS MY...

This
Beautiful
Black
Brother
Divinely dipped in ethereal excellence
Makes mountains move when it comes to
Me
He calls me his
Quintessential queen
His
Thick-up Thug
His
Gorgeous Gangsta
His
Inspirational ink that "Phlows" passion through his
pen
He no longer craves
Fhyisical food
Because
The sustenance of my soul's sugary sweetness
Purposefully penetrates him with all the
nourishment he needs to aNnihilate nations
And I
Graciously grant him all my glorious givings
Because
He is my
Kingdom's keeper
My
Perfect prophesy
My
Rock-hard Rameses
My
Metaphysical movement

SPILLIN DA PHIYAH

He's the
Rhythmical reason behind every lusciously, lustfully,
love-filled lyric
He has
Feloniously fanned my ferocious fire twenty times
since Tuesday
Using
Nothing More
Than
Nouns and Metaphors
We are
Each other's
Secret soliloquy
Hushed hearts harbored among the breeze
Such a torridly tantalizing treat
Cunningly candid conversations make our voracious
verbal exchanges complete
This juicy juxtaposition
Has us both weak....wantonly wishin'
For opulent overdoses of
This
Magical mojo
This
Diabolical dripping
This
Exemplary ecstasy
This
Alluringly affable affair
This
Beautiful
Black
Brother
Who moves massive mountains
For I
His Quintessential queen
Really GETS me

EDITED VERSIONS OF MY SOUL

So he can get IT
Anytime....

November 23, 2014

SPILLIN DA PHIYAH

OFFICIALLY OFF THE MARKET

The last tenant moved out in the wee hours of the
morning
Politely backed the U-Haul up to the side door and
proceeded to pack up half of the "forever" we'd
planned together
Said he'd outgrown the cramped quarters and
needed more space to move around
I tried to negotiate a new contract with him
Told him I'd get rid of some of my shoes so he'd
have more closet space
Told him I'd stop hogging all the sheets at night
Told him I'd be so quiet he'd forget I was even in the
house
Just please....please.....please baby
With a cherry on top
Please....don't go

But apparently he'd been searching for a new place
to lay his head for awhile
Because he'd already paid his deposit and his new
"landlord" was patiently awaiting his arrival
Please baby....with a cherry on top....don't go
He said "sorry Love..."
And shut the door behind him

FOR SALE:
One heart
Bruised and battered
Torn and tattered
Former tenant caused major damage
Left walls covered in blood spatter
Much work needs to be done
And I'm not sure how long it'll take to repair

EDITED VERSIONS OF MY SOUL

But it's a beautiful fixer-upper
Long as you got some time to spare

And so there it sat
Cobwebs beginning to form in every crevice and
corner
As I patiently awaited new love's arrival
While secretly still hoping for old love's return
Oh a few prospects breezed through from
time-to-time
But they either lacked the patience required to turn
this old rundown shack into a beautiful new
mansion
Or I just didn't trust them enough to maintain the
necessary upkeep
I began to lose all hope that these 4 walls would
ever again know how it feels to be filled with love
And so, in the wee hours of the morning,
I dejectedly decided to take down my....

"Excuse me Miss
I hope this space is still available.
I should've come through months ago, but whenever
I saw someone else checking it out, I'd lose
hope...believing I'd missed my chance.
But seeing that it's still empty,
I'd love to come inside and take a look around..."

Past experiences had me primed to say no...
Yet something told me that this time...it would be
different
Anxiety took over as he stepped inside
And as he slowly, yet calmly, perused the severe
wear and tear,
Fear began to speak loudly in my ear...

SPILLIN DA PHIYAH

Too much damage has been done
He's going to think it's too bruised and battered
Too torn and tattered
He's going to notice that the walls require too much
paint to cover up all the blood spatter

I quietly said,
"Much work needs to be done
And I'm not sure how long it'll take to repair;
But it's a beautiful fixer-upper
Long as you got some time to spare."

He took one last look around,
Then he looked at me,
Smiled,
And asked....
"So when can I move in?"

March 23, 2015

EDITED VERSIONS OF MY SOUL

QUALITY TIME

I cherish moments like these.
They come so few and far in between now.
You know how it is sometimes…
We start off talking every day;
Life takes over;
And before you know it,
Months have gone by since I was last in
Your presence.

But today…
It's time you and I reconnect with each other.
I need You to speak to me.
I need You to speak IN to me.

Your Words ebb through my spirit like the tide,
forever washing away any doubt that I've ever had
about your true feelings for me.

No matter how deep my pain you always manage
to wrap my heart tenderly in Your palms and
massage each pain away, as though your fingers
are intricately caressing every piano keyed
transgression.

When the troubles of this world become far too
much
for me to bear alone, You open Your arms to me and
I
boldly run into them every time,
unashamed and unconcerned about
who may be watching or what they may be saying.

You are my rock.

SPILLIN DA PHIYAH

You are my strength.
You are my footprints in the sand.
You are my Do-Re-Mi-Fa-So-La-Ti-Do…

Oh!
How marvelous you are to me!

With You I am so free…

So if it's ok with You,
can we
please pretend like we never lost contact
and pick up where we left off?

Because

As I'm sure You already know…

We have A LOT of catching up to do.

August 5, 2014

EDITED VERSIONS OF MY SOUL

REMOVED

How dare you expose me
I wasn't ready
I didn't ask for any of this
I didn't ask for any of….you
I was perfectly fine (for the most part)
To remain hidden in my hurt
Pressed down in my pain
Deadlocked in my disappointment
It felt…dare I admit…safe
No chance of getting caught up
No chance of being let down
No way of tripping and falling
Face first
Into love's disrespectful grasp
I was perfectly fine (for the most part)
Being alone
And then here you came
And proved me a liar
Got me realizing that (for the most part)
I wasn't fine at all
Got me realizing precisely what I was missing along
This…this-ness
This…you-ness
And now I'm begging you to please
Release me from this rain
Purge me from this pain
Deliver me from my despair
Walls crumbled
Heart opened
Mask shattered
I have tripped
And fallen
Face first

SPILLIN DA PHIYAH

Into love's all forgiving arms
The difference?
This time
I think I'm ready

July 1, 2014

TIME WELL SPENT

These moments we share
Away from the world, away from prying eyes
Where the only sounds that break the silence
Are our heartbeats and contented sighs

Bring me pleasure immeasurable
And I find myself counting the ways
That I can squeeze another second out of every
possible minute
And add 24 more hours to these special days

In this whole grand space time continuum
Did our souls fleetingly touch in each other's
dreams
Because it truly blows my mind how we've found in
each other
A connection that keeps us joined at the seams

So despite the circumstances that keep us apart
Let's just enjoy these brief moments together
Because until we both make some very pertinent
decisions
The next time we touch each other....may be never

August 29, 2014

SPILLIN DA PHIYAH

WHAT A COINCIDENCE

The husband you're fervently praying to God
To send into your life
Is the very same man who's fervently praying to
God
To present to him his wife

As you're praying for him to be the lover
And protector of your heart
He's praying for you to allow him
To prove himself from the very start

You want him to understand the strength you have
To make it on your own
And he wants you to understand
That you no longer have to do it all alone

You're praying to God to bless you with your King
Who's more than willing to commit
He's praying to God to bless him with his Queen
Who's more than willing to submit

You're passionate and staunch in what you believe
So he must embrace your spirit to fight
And he's perfectly fine with that
Long as you realize that that doesn't mean you
ALWAYS have to be right

You're ready for your Jacob
Willing to put in work for the long haul
And he's ready to climb the highest mountain for his
Rachel
Just be ready to catch him IF he might fall

EDITED VERSIONS OF MY SOUL

So keep fervently praying because God IS listening
But you still got some work to do
Because the husband you're praying for is preparing
himself for his wife
And let's pray that she's you

August 28, 2015

SPILLIN DA PHIYAH

YOU COULD CARE LESS

I want so badly to turn these lights off
To hide from you what the many years of
Childbearing, macaroni and cheese and plain ol' life
Has done to my once eye-popping, heart-stopping,
jaw-dropping body.

I don't want you to see that my once juicy, perky
breasts,
The same ones that used to stand upright on their
own, full at attention,
Unassisted by the awkward grips of underwire and
push-up bras,
Now seem to hang lower than a cumulus cloud
preparing to burst forth with summer rains.

I don't want you to see that my once smooth, full
derriere,
The same one that seemed to keep grooving long
after I'd stopped moving,
That made MANY men long to be the jeans that
were so lovingly caressing it,
Now sag like the jeans of those young men who
sadly have no clue what their waist size is.

I don't want you to see that my once sexy thighs,
The same ones that made any pants I wore look as
though the fabric were molded to my skin,
That made MANY men rub their hands in sheer
anticipation of just the THOUGHT of getting
between them,
Now do nothing more than rub together as I walk.

Just sad.

EDITED VERSIONS OF MY SOUL

Please…..I'm begging you…..let me turn off these
lights.
Darkness makes my silhouette look so much sexier.
Or at least allow me to keep my shirt on………ok?
And you say……

No.

And as embarrassed tears begin to pool in my eyes,
You kiss them away and ask me:

"Why would you not want me to see these beautiful
breasts?
The same ones that you unabashedly loved and
nourished our babies from?
That would lull them into the deepest doze as soon
as you rested their weary heads upon them.
Now I drink from them, never full from that same
love, nourishment and pillow-soft rest.

Why would you not want me to see that beautiful
behind?
The same one that continues to put me in a trance
every time you dance?
That makes THIS man long to be the jeans lucky
enough to caress it on the daily.
I now use these hands of mine to grip that butt and
pull your body closer to my desire.

Why would you not want me to see these sexy
thighs?
The same ones our children would wrap their arms
around for support after a fall?
That makes THIS man's nature rise in anticipation
from just the THOUGHT of lying between them.

SPILLIN DA PHIYAH

I now get to do that every night as our moans split
the atmosphere.

So blessed.

So no.....we're leaving the lights on.
You're so much sexier when I can see what's in
front of me.
So please allow me to see what the many years of
Bearing our beautiful children,
Meals prepared from our kitchen with love
And our plain ol' God-blessed life
Has now done to your life-giving, blessed-living,
fire-delivering body.
You see, I could care less about society and their
opinions about beauty.
Beauty is in the eye of the beholder....
So come let me hold you....Beauty.

Written: December 2013
Revised: November 2015

...HE LOVES ME NOT

SPILLIN DA PHIYAH

BROKEN RECORD

As I turn on our street my heart starts to flutter
And I begin wishing on every single star
That as I draw ever closer to our home
I will not see your car

I pray that I can walk through the door
And inhale the presence of peace
And exhale the stench of utter dread
As I prepare for sweet release

You see, you and I sit among these walls
Sharing the very same space
But something is not sitting well with me
Because even though this is MY home, I feel out of
place

I constantly drown in my feelings
While I embrace the attitude that you wear
Your silence rings loud and clear
You no longer want to be here

Me: "Is everything ok? Are you mad at me?
Baby, tell me did I do something wrong?"
You: "I just don't feel like talking"
But 2 minutes later, I hear you on the phone

Talking loud, laughing louder
How? When you just dismissed me like I was dust?
You look straight through my crying eyes
Straight through my hurt and disgust

You're getting dressed while making plans
To once again leave me alone

EDITED VERSIONS OF MY SOUL

Among these same four walls
Within this increasingly uncomfortable home

Like a song that just won't get out your head
This scenario is stuck on repeat
Because I've always been made to believe
That I need a man in my life to make me feel
complete

So now seeing your car in the driveway
It's just a constant reminder to me
That as sick as I am of living in this pain
I'm too much of a punk to ever set me free

Written: December 2013
Revised November 2015

SPILLIN DA PHIYAH

COLE....YOU STUPID

It appears you're a glutton for punishment
Or maybe you're just a freak like that
Ohhhhh
So you DO like getting beat to a pulp, huh?
Forgive me please
See, I know I'm grasping at straws here
But I'm just trying to understand
What it is that makes you keep falling for the
Okie doke
Like being trampled on the first 1,527 times wasn't
enough for you
OH NO!
You keep running back for more and more....and
more and more and more
Wow...you are truly dumb as burnt toast
I am SOOOO sick and tired of you and your
stupidity
I KEEP telling you
Yo...for real...chill out
Leave love and ALL its foolishness alone
Because all love has EVER done is hurt you
Oh but you grown tho
So can't nobody tell you nuthin cuz you think you
know EVERY thing
So you open wide your doors
Swoon over a couple words
On the "pages" of a "book"
And once again you become caught up in the
promise of "maybe"
Only to get pimp slapped with the cold hard reality
THAT LOVE REALLY DON'T LOVE YOU
DUMMY

EDITED VERSIONS OF MY SOUL

And now here you come
With that snifflin and cryin and scrambled egg on
your face
Expecting me to dry your tears
And lick your bruises
And slap a Band-Aid on your wounds
And guess what?
I always do
Because if I don't step in to save you from you
You liable to kill yo'self
What IS it gonna to take for you to FINALLY learn
That I AM THE BRAINS in this little operation?
It's MY job to think for the BOTH of us
Because you are seriously too stupid to know any
better
Just pump blood and leave all the THINKING to
me...ok
Because when YOU hurt
I hurt
And my tolerance for pain decreases every time you
break
So stop this once and for all
We don't need love
We got each other

October 2, 2015

SPILLIN DA PHIYAH

FOREVER MEANS FOREVER...RIGHT?

She said she was ready
She better be
Most of her sista/friends
Were already 20 years in
Some were working on round 2
A few were already on 3 and 4
And here she was
40
One man-child drenched in a separate legacy
Attached to her hip
Yet SHE still bears her same name
Now ain't that a shame
Mortgages and mothers-in-law
Cheeks filled with way too much sugar and
Choices between Disneyland and the backyard
For this year's family vacation
Dogs
Cats
Goldfish
Iguanas
All dreams of her "Forever"
Had somehow eluded her all these years

So OF COURSE when "Hmm...Maybe" came
along
She jumped on "Possibility's" train
I mean hey
Why risk "Never" coming back around again
Right
But alas, he, "Perhaps," wasn't ready to be her
"Forever"
And apparently no amount of

EDITED VERSIONS OF MY SOUL

Praying or
Prodding or
Pressing or
Pouting or
Please baby, baby please
Prepared him for THIS day

THIS was supposed to be her walk into
"FINALLY"
Through her white picket fence
Into "I never gotta take out the trash myself again"
Into "I never gotta pump my own gas again"
Into "Thank you Jesus…now I won't grow old and
die alone"
Into "Happily Ever After"
Into "FINALLY…I have someone who will love
me…Forever"

Man
What the hell kinda sorry fairytale is
THIS
"Forever" didn't whisk her away into the sunset
Like she'd "forever" envisioned
Oh no
Instead
She remains seated here
Alone
In her "Frantic Reality"
And as if punched in the gut
With the closed fist of "Clarity"
She comes to the frightful conclusion that
"Perhaps"
Here
Where she sits now
Alone
Is in fact

SPILLIN DA PHIYAH

Her
"Forever"

July 15, 2014

EDITED VERSIONS OF MY SOUL

HAPPY MISERY

I've stunned her into silence
I feel her watching me walk away
She just can't believe
The news she's received
She has no words to say

It was never my intent to hurt her
Where she stands now, I've stood many times before
The lies and deceit
Pain stuck on repeat
Heartbreak that cuts down to the core

She calls me a bitch and a home wrecker
She asks me how I didn't know
I tell her he never ONCE mentioned her name
But she still sees ME as the blame
To her, I'm nothing but a ho

He's playing us BOTH for fools
He's putting us BOTH through hell
And the tears we BOTH weep
Prove we're BOTH in too deep
And in a few months, my belly will start to swell

But the one thing we BOTH can agree on
Is that HE needs to make a decision TODAY
Whether it's her or it's me
We can BOTH plainly see
That NEITHER of us is strong enough to walk away

SPILLIN DA PHIYAH

We BOTH have too much to lose
So if he's refuses to choose
This "happy misery" is where we'll BOTH stay

November 3, 2014

EDITED VERSIONS OF MY SOUL

THE END

My soul was a seed
Fresh and new
Just born into the complications
Of this thing called love
And then you came along
My knight in shining armor
And released me from the earth
Like a dove

My soul became a bud
You showered me with
Your waters of attention
And affection
But just as quickly
You crushed the petals of my heart
With the hand of pain
And rejection

My soul is now withered and dry
No longer affected
By the sun of your eyes
The waters of your smile
The care of your touch
I think back to the day
We first met
And I wonder now, if possibly, it was I
Who loved too much

December 1998

SPILLIN DA PHIYAH

THEM

How dare you turn me into one of "them"
One of "them" lost women who once had a mind of
her very own
But who'd now rather put up with bullshit than face
the prospect of being forever alone
Inside a weak little girl...making believe that she's
full grown

How could you turn me into one of "them"
One of "them" mind-boggled chicks, constantly
crazed and obsessin'
Always cryin' and stressin'
Heart breakin' with each new confession
Once considered myself a Queen
Now you got me feelin' "less than"

What did I do to you to make you turn me into one
of "them"
One of "them" type females me and my girls used to
sit and talk about
One who accepts the excuses and foolishness rather
than throw his no-good behind out
Funny how quickly self-confidence can be
diminished into shame and self-doubt

Why was I so willing to allow you to turn me into
one of "them"
Was it the promises you made
Was it that good lovin' you laid
The fact that you keep all the bills paid
Or maybe I'm just plain ol' afraid

I don't wanna be myself and the pickings out here
are few

EDITED VERSIONS OF MY SOUL

You know how hard it is being single when
everybody's boo'd up but you
So you keep hanging in there, praying he'll change
cuz....what else can you really do

So I'll thank y'all kindly not to judge me
Making me feel worse than I already am
Y'all can say whatever you like because at this point,
I no longer give a damn
Yeah I'm sure you see me as one of "them" pitiful
chicks
But hey....at least I can say I got a man

March 8, 2015

SPILLIN DA PHIYAH

UNSPOKEN

Once upon a midnight lonely
While I thought about you only
Reading many a long and serious letter
I've received from you
As I read them, my eyes crying
My heart's broken, damn near dying
Cuz it thinks that you've been lying
Lying to it all these years
Yes it knows that you've been lying
Lying to it all these years
Now I wipe away my tears

As I sit there, my mind dazin
I see nothing, my eyes glazin
And my feelings are amazin
Cuz I don't know why they're there
I really wish I was still with you
But with all the hurt I've been through
All the pain and heartaches too
Could I go through that again
All the cheating and different women
Could I survive all that again
What do I really have to gain

And then I realize I don't need you
I don't want you, I don't miss you
There's no way that I could go through
All the things I have before
Some things just go best unspoken
This relationship is broken
I've been treated like some token
And I ain't taking it no more

EDITED VERSIONS OF MY SOUL

I refuse to be your hobby
So I'm walking out the door
To be seen forever no more

Circa: July 1994

MY PHLOW =

OUR TRUTHS

EDITED VERSIONS OF MY SOUL

BLINDED BY THE FACTS

"Wait on the Lord: be of good courage, and He shall
strengthen thine heart: wait I say, on the Lord."
Psalm 27:14.

What's a logical amount of time to wait on
anything?
For example, the bus?
How about a cab?
Or to be seen by the doctor?

Perhaps those particular questions aren't quite
logical to ask.
You see, as long as you have the bus schedule,
And you're in the proper place at the proper time,
You ALREADY KNOW that eventually the bus will
arrive to take you to your destination.

SPILLIN DA PHIYAH

You called a cab to come pick you up;

And while the cab still hasn't arrived yet,

You're not worried, because your call has been

logged and

You ALREADY KNOW that eventually the cab will

arrive to take you to your destination.

Your doctor's appointment was at 8am.

It's now 9am and you have yet to be seen.

You probably won't make a fuss though because

even though the doctor is running behind,

You ALREADY KNOW that because you've been

scheduled to be seen, you SHALL be seen.

The bus hasn't arrived yet.

The cab hasn't pulled up to your door yet.

The doctor STILL hasn't called your name yet.

Yet,

EDITED VERSIONS OF MY SOUL

We continue to sit….and wait.

Why?

Because we know that if we are patient,

And continue to wait,

EVENTUALLY, we'll FINALLY receive what

we've been waiting on:

The bus will FINALLY pull up to your stop;

The cab will FINALLY blow the horn for you;

And the doctor will FINALLY see you now.

Our waiting FINALLY paid off!

Patience was SHO NUFF a virtue!

Thing is…

It was EASY waiting on those things, right?

Because even though we couldn't SEE them

RIGHT THEN,

SPILLIN DA PHIYAH

We maintained our FAITH in the FACT that

No matter HOW long we may have to sit and wait

for them,

EVENTUALLY, they SHALL show up, right?

So then….

Why can't we maintain that exact,

Same,

Unwavering FAITH when it comes to waiting on

The Lord?

Because right now….

We don't SEE Him.

What we DO see though, are the

COLD,

HARD,

FACTS!

You lost your job.

EDITED VERSIONS OF MY SOUL

The bills are due.

The car is acting up.

The chir'en done lost their ever-loving minds.

Ain't no food in the house.

No money coming in to provide.

Your head hurts.

Your back hurts.

Your feet hurt.

Your heart hurts.

Because you're tired.

Tired of watching;

Tired of waiting;

Tired of struggling;

Tired of crying;

Tired of not knowing when change is FINALLY

coming.

And,

If you're not afraid to be TOTALLY honest with

yourself right now,

You're even tired….of praying.

You're just plain, ol' tired.

But wait a minute now….

Haven't you been in THIS place before?

And hasn't the Lord ALWAYS shown up?

Just like the bus?

Just like the cab?

Just like the doctor?

So then WHY in God's Name are we trippin' when

the FACT is

We ALREADY KNOW that the Lord has

ALREADY handled

EVERYTHANG!

And we are good to go!

We just can't SEE it yet.

EDITED VERSIONS OF MY SOUL

So in the meantime,

Pour yourself a nice, cool glass of sweet tea,

Kick your feet up,

And relax.

And get ready.

Because He's already on the way…

July 20, 2014

SPILLIN DA PHIYAH

CAN SOMEBODY THROW ME A TOWEL

PLEASE?

Bills to the left of me

Bills to the right

Water bill

Phone bill

Car insurance

Light

Drowning under grocery bill

Drowning under rent

I tend to keep it all internalized

So forgive me for this vent

Haven't worked in 8 months

EDITED VERSIONS OF MY SOUL

Trying hard to survive

Trying hard to remain grateful

Every day I'm still alive

Cuz every day I'm still alive

That's another day to try

But every day I wanna cry

Because my well has gone dry

No need to ask God "why"

Because the answer's always "why not"

I just wanna be able to pay these bills

And afford to get my child's hair cut

That ain't askin' for a lot

But here I be

Sinking ever deeper in this murky pile of debt

I know my Savior cometh, but I do wish He'd hurry

SPILLIN DA PHIYAH

Because I still don't see my life raft yet....

                                    December 28, 2014

EDITED VERSIONS OF MY SOUL

CHAIN REACTION

I'm not sure how much longer I'll be able

To hold my breath;

Waiting for you to decide to let go of whatever it is

That has you rooted in your shame.

Confined.

Trapped.

Chained.

Why do you refuse to be free?

Then again,

I guess the same can be asked of me.

You see, try as I might to break through the surface,

Bob just a wee bit higher,

Get my head just above water so I can finally

exhale,

I continue to give all my power to the "things" of

this world,

Allowing the weights to pull me back down.

Complacency is so easy, isn't it?

But is it beneficial to our health?

Physically.

Emotionally.

Mentally.

Spiritually.

Because of our individual demons,

Our STRONGHOLDS,

Neither of us can be everything we both possess

The power to be for each other.

You're reaching out your hand to me,

EDITED VERSIONS OF MY SOUL

Struggling to save me from the murky swamp of

My misery.

And I hold the key to the one thing that can

relinquish you from

Your shackled and shattered past….

My heart.

So on the count of 3,

Let's break these locks and decide

Once and for all,

That even though our pasts were born unto us,

They will never live to dictate our present.

This situation is dire,

And our future is at stake.

It's now…or never…

SPILLIN DA PHIYAH

1…

2…

3…

August 13, 2014

EDITED VERSIONS OF MY SOUL

DON'T BE TALKIN' BOUT MY MAMA
To All My Mothers

You peeped her steez soon as she walked through

the door

Gorgeous face, thick waist, but ugly seeps from her

pores

You can see you're gonna have to put your foot

down once more

Cuz just like all the others, you've met this chick

here before

Nothing substantial to say but she keeps an attitude

She thinks she radiates strength when in fact she's

just rude

Walkin' 'round on eggshells cuz you can never

detect her mood

Relationships end quick because of the bitterness

she exudes

SPILLIN DA PHIYAH

Everything is an argument and she's always down to

fight

Please don't think you'll ever win because she

ALWAYS has to be right

She wears the "stink face" morning, noon and night

You thought your son had some sense but

apparently he ain't too bright

As a matter fact, it's obvious he's lost his

ever-loving mind

All the women on this earth and this is all he could

find?

He used to have dreams and was constantly on his

grind

But the kiss of this spider must've rendered him

blind

Swelling his ego while she sucks him dry

EDITED VERSIONS OF MY SOUL

So trapped in her spell, he no longer knows the truth
from a lie

Walk away from her? He may as well not even try

Cuz he simply returns to the foolishness soon as
there's a mist in her eye

The great King he was becoming is a thing of the
past

Ignorant in his lust and the switch of her ass

Whatever you gotta do, you know you better do it
fast

Cuz you'll be ice-skating in hell before you see this
mistake last

Your boy will regain his crown no matter what you
gotta do

Separate him from the devil and the hell she's
putting him through

SPILLIN DA PHIYAH

As long as he's with HER, nothing will change, and

you know it's true

Because other mothers have had to rescue their sons

from you

August 30, 2015

EDITED VERSIONS OF MY SOUL

I THINK I HATE MY SON

I think I hate my son

Not for the child he is

But for the man he could become

You see in him, I see a whole lotta you

So since you good for nothing, will that be his fate

too

Will he develop your laziness

And all your sorry ways

Will he make promises to be there

And then not show up for days

Will he always try his best and do everything he can

To use you as an example of what not to be as a

man

Or is he just another po' black boy destined to be

Not a product of his dreams, but of this world that

he sees

SPILLIN DA PHIYAH

My son, my son, my poor, poor son

My whack, sorry, triflin', ol' good fuh nuthin' son

I see his grades slip

I see the smoke from the grass

I see the bevy of females lined up to grant him a

free pass

Treating him like a king

Like his little ding-a-ling is so sweet

Until he does what he came to do and makes a hasty

retreat

Nine months going once, twice, three, four times

A girl, then a boy, another girl and boy in the line

And now I gotta take on the same role as your mom

And be a better father than our deadbeat son

These girls' tears burn my ears as they once again

cry

"Why can't he do right?! Why he always gotta lie?!

Why can't he be there for his kids, especially his

57

son?!"

Well how does a man be a dad when he never had

one

I hate him for the position he might put me in

I done been through this crap with you

And now he's takin' me thru it again

Four different baby mamas and ain't married to

NONE

My ho'in', lyin', cheatin', ol' good fuh nuthin' son

He ain't got no job or no hope for tomorrow

He can't gimme nuthin' cuz he always gotta borrow

So fulla promise but no kinda ambition

Unless he sniffin out the ladies

Which seems to be his only mission

Bouncin' from one woman's house to the next

Leavin' each one all the more confused and

perplexed

Oh he said that he love you? Sweetie he just told her

the same thing

He asked you to marry him?! Well where the hell is

the ring?

See right now, I'm having me a horrible case of déjà

vu

Cuz instead of seeing my son, all I see is you

But let me pause for a second, cuz I'm really not

being fair

The truth of this matter has finally become clear

See there's a perfectly good reason why I wouldn't

give him your first name

Cuz although you two look alike, you'll NEVER be

one in the same

And just like the stigma that's been placed upon

every black male

My child can't succeed if I've already set him up to

fail

And I know that the responsibility first lies with me

EDITED VERSIONS OF MY SOUL

Cuz how can I push him into the future if I can't set
my past free

Still angry with you, yet HE catches my wrath

You abandon him, I neglect him; now you do the
math

But since it was YOU who chose to walk out on
him again

It's YOU who's gonna suffer for this in the end

This child is destined for greatness, he's worthy of
the best

And now that I've FINALLY let you go, he can now
progress

Into the image of God that's already been planned

This strong, highly-favored blessing of a man

My son, my son, I love my son

For the change he SHALL become

Despite the one he came from

SPILLIN DA PHIYAH

Written: April 2009
Revised: September 2012
2nd Revision: November 2015

EDITED VERSIONS OF MY SOUL

KEEPS ON SLIPPIN'

I need more of you.

I hate your elusiveness.

Please stop teasing me.

You're never enough.

Searching but never finding

Extra grains of you.

Every missed second...

Every single lost hour....

I placed blame on you.

But yet you blamed me.

Said if I budget better

You'll always be here.

SPILLIN DA PHIYAH

Well where are you now?

I'm here crying out for you

But you don't respond.

How does that song go?

"Time keeps on slippin'....slippin'..."

I feel you slippin'....

Is that the right time?

It's not earlier than that?

Where DID the time go?

I thought we had time....

Thought you'd always wait for me....

Sigh....guess I was wrong.

March 13, 2015

EDITED VERSIONS OF MY SOUL

LOOK AWAY

I wonder if you're able to look through me

Deep into my soul and really see

How fake I truly am

All you see is my forever smile

Not realizing that for quite a while

I've been forever dying inside

The constant jokes I crack...all for a laugh

Would probably make you cry if you only knew the

half

Sometimes I feel my life ain't worth a damn

Please....don't stare at me for too long

I don't want you to figure out what's really wrong

I still have secrets I'd like to continue to hide

SPILLIN DA PHIYAH

Don't you worry about me

My reflection is all you need to see

Because right now....all I have left IS my pride

April 3, 2015

EDITED VERSIONS OF MY SOUL

ME VERSUS SHE

Happy to be free

Happy to be me

But who in the world is this

Fat chick starin' at me

She looks real familiar

Like I've seen her before

But she looks so different

I really can't be sure

She's starin' at me me so hard

And each glance is longer than the last

And she looks like she needs to go

Standin' there nekked

Like she got it goin' on

But what she really need to do

Is put her clothes back on

On a seven day fast

SPILLIN DA PHIYAH

Her breasts are all saggy

And there's cellulite on her thighs

Maybe she shoulda had the burger

WITHOUT the shake and the fries

Everybody says she's beautiful

But they tell such lies

They're just tryin' not to make her cry

No matter which way she turns

She still looks like a whale

I swear if fatness was a crime

She'd be up under the jail

She need to be ashamed

For allowing herself to get that big

And then she got the nerve

To try and blame it on her kid

Just look at all that food

She got piled on her plate

She's GOT to know that's why

EDITED VERSIONS OF MY SOUL

She's so overweight

She sneaks in the kitchen

After everyone's asleep

And eats her insecurities

Until she's got em buried deep

No more feeling fat

No more low self-esteem

She swallowed all that down

With the pizza and ice cream

No more feeling unattractive

No more acne or bad hair

Cuz the greasy fried chicken

Shows her tenderness and care

No more extra half-a-stomach

Or doing the "jumpy-dance"

Trying hard to suck it all in

As she fastens her pants

No more feeling unworthy

SPILLIN DA PHIYAH

Or ugly or plain

No more hurt or embarrassment

Or sadness or pain

She can't seem to find love

Anyplace else

So she chooses to stick with the

Cookies and chips on her shelf

Happy to be free

Happy to just be

But none of us will EVER be TRULY happy

Until "me" learns to love "she"

Written: November 2009
Revised November 2013

EDITED VERSIONS OF MY SOUL

MY BAD Y'ALL

To all the guys I've loved before
I owe every last one of you
An apology
And I mean that sincerely
From the very bottom of the same heart
That you each ripped to shreds
See even though it was YOU
Who cheated on ME
And YOU who always made ME cry
And YOU who continued to spoon feed ME
Little appetizers of your love
Because you very quickly discovered that I was a
"cheap date"
And would never see myself worthy of demanding
The full course meal of your commitment and
respect
I understand now
That it is I who inevitably forced your hand
I erroneously placed the entire burden
Of MY happiness
On YOUR shoulders
I expected YOU
To be ALL of the things
That my father never was to me
I expected YOU
To lose yourself in ME
Just as I'd disappeared into you
I expected YOU
To forget you had a life
Before ME
Just as I'd suddenly developed
A severe case of amnesia for you
When you moved, I moved

SPILLIN DA PHIYAH

Just like that
And I expected you to do the same
I expected YOU
To be MY savior
I expected each one of YOU
To be the one to unpack ALL of the baggage
That I was still carrying
From each of my previous "road trips"
I expected YOU to be
Perfect
And anything less was unacceptable
And no ONE person
Deserves THAT kind of pressure
Placed upon them
And for all of that
I am deeply sorry
By NO means am I condoning or accepting
Any hurtful thing that any of you ever did to me
But I CAN accept the fact that because my lifelong
insecurities
Kept ME from loving ME properly
None of YOU could love me properly
So to all the guys I've loved before
Thank you for indirectly teaching me
The TRUE meaning of love
By showing me that I can't expect
ANY man to give me the
Love, acceptance and respect that I crave
If I haven't even given it to myself

April 25, 2014

EDITED VERSIONS OF MY SOUL

NEVER BEEN

I wonder how different I'd be today
Had I been a "Daddy's Girl"
Would I have been the apple of your eye
Would I have been the nucleus of your world

Would you have been the first to hold me
Fresh from my mother's abyss
Would you have wrapped me in the warmth of your
arms
And given me my very first kiss

Would you have walked the floor til I stopped
crying
And watched me as I slept
Would you have been grinning from ear-to-ear
As I came towards you with my first steps

Would you have shed a tear my first day of school
As I unsuredly let go of your sleeve
Would you have stood and watched me at the
classroom door
Until the teacher nicely asked you to leave

Would you have come to all my orchestra and choir
concerts
Would you have cheered me on at my spelling bees
Would you have bought me candy and toys for
always making the Honor Roll
I'm sure you would've been pleased

Would you have taught me how to drive
Jokingly feigning whiplash, every time I stopped
the car with a jerk

SPILLIN DA PHIYAH

Would you have spoiled me rotten, buying me
everything I wanted
Or would you have made me go out and work

Would you have asked all my boyfriends
What their intentions with me were, daring them to
tell you a lie
Would you have threatened to buss a cap straight in
their ass
If they ever made your "baby girl" cry

Would you have embarrassed me at my high school
graduation
All in the aisle with the video camera, just yelling
so loud
With tears in your eyes, chest swole to bursting
Because your "baby girl" has made you so proud

Would I have used you as my prototype
For the man who could've entered my life
Would I have wanted to marry a man just like you
I could've made the perfect wife

Years creep by, questions still abound
And I have no idea where you could be
For a while I was even angry with my mother
Because I thought she was keeping you from me

And even with all the questions that I had
The greatest wonderment of all
Is even though you were never here with me
You mean to tell me you couldn't even call

You never wondered what I looked like
If any of our features were the same
Do you even know when my birthday is

EDITED VERSIONS OF MY SOUL

Do you even know my middle name

41 years of unanswered questions
And still no closer to the truth
Until one fine day, like The Great Whodini
You just appear……clean out of the blue

All of the wonders that I've wondered about
I can finally ask you, now that you're here
But to my great surprise, not only don't I ask them
I realize I no longer care

You see, nothing you could've said would've
changed my life
Or the path I chose to take
Because I needed these things from you GROWING
UP
And as a GROWN woman now, it's too late

I wish I could say I wanted a relationship with you
But sadly, I really don't
And as I put the finishing touches on this poem
It'll make 4 years since last we spoke

It's quite alright though, I've survived without you
thus far
And I'll continue to do so til the very end
Because even though it might've been nice to have
been your "baby girl"
I can't miss being something I've never been

Written: December 19, 2013
Revised: November 2015

74

SPILLIN DA PHIYAH

NEW AND IMPROVED

The look on your face is priceless
This new brand of Tiffany isn't sitting too well with
you I see
Too much time has passed
She's had time to think
Time to digress
Time to reassess
Time to reprocess
Time to reinvest
In herself
However, it appears you were counting on
reconnecting
With the Tiffany of old
Desperate Tiffany
Gullible Tiffany
Vulnerable Tiffany
Weak Tiffany
The Tiffany that hung on your every word
No matter how absurd
Because to her
They were the sweetest lies she'd ever heard
You swore you had her heart back in your clutches
As soon as you whispered in her ear
"Baby....I've missed you"
The Tiffany of old
Would've melted into a puddle of jubilation
Her mind once again locked in her caged
stupification
Completely forgetting all of the prior devastation
That propelled her soul into utter annihilation
Ah but alas that Tiffany of old is no more
She has allowed her system to be upgraded and
rebooted

EDITED VERSIONS OF MY SOUL

And you are now face-to-face with Tiffany 2.0
Confident Tiffany
Astute Tiffany
Secure Tiffany
Stable Tiffany
Who, instead of melting into that said puddle of
jubilation
Looked you deep into your eyes
Smiled and sighed
And said,
"Instead of MISSING me,
How bout you MISS me instead?"
Did ya catch that?

January 22, 2014

SPILLIN DA PHIYAH

REEEEWIIIIIIND

THEY say everything happens for a reason
And that some situations are only for a season
Is this true? Or are THEY just appeasin'?

See, if I had done ANYTHING differently
I wonder would I still be
The same ol' Tiffany?

From dropping outta college
Way back in 90-fo'
To chasing behind every no count man
I ain't even wit' no mo'

From trying so hard to fit in
That I sometimes missed standing out
To every opportunity I allowed to escape my grasp
Because my faith wasn't strong as my doubt

From spreading my legs way more
Than I've ever lifted my hands
To never questioning those things
I just couldn't understand

From being arrested
To double homelessness
From "baby daddy" drama
To sinking deeper in distress

Every single trial
I've ever been through
I swore I'd die in my sorrow
But God already knew

EDITED VERSIONS OF MY SOUL

The scars have disappeared
And I no longer feel the burns
Because my life is simply a miniseries
Of lessons I have learned

Where I am right now
Is where I'm supposed to be
Yes I'm still in the struggle
But God's grace and mercy keeps my mind free

So yes in most circumstances
A "do-over" would sho nuff be swell
But for now, I'll just leave things the way that they
are
That way, I've always got a story to tell

December 9, 2014

SPILLIN DA PHIYAH

SHE LOVES ME

"She" wants "Me" to look at her
Without scrutinizing every single scar
Without dissing every single dent in her skin
Without frowning at every single flaw

See "she" thinks she is beautiful
And she wants "me" to see that too
But "she" is only a reflection of "me"
She has no idea what I've been through

Teased mercilessly all through school
Y'all know how kids are, bluntly mean and cruel
Limited creative insults, but never underestimate the
sting
"WIT' YA FAT SELF" tacked at the end of simple
attacks can bring
Always picked last for teams
"Man! Her fat self gon' make us lose!" they'd say
So I'd go all the way to the back of the line and
begin to pray
"Before it's my turn Lord, please let the bell ring
That way everybody's happy because I won't have
to do anything"

It's bad enough all the cute boys would look past
me
To all the pretty "red" or skinnier girls sitting right
behind me
When my mother lost her job, she could no longer
afford
To at least buy me all the cute clothes and shoes
From Sears and Montgomery Ward
So now not only am I fat, my gear is less than fly

EDITED VERSIONS OF MY SOUL

Many of my weekends were spent at home
Where I'd eat and cry, and bitterly ask God,
"Why?!"
Why wasn't I born lighter? Why couldn't I be
skinny?
I see beauty all AROUND me, but not necessarily
IN me"
Low self-esteem began to bury my soul
It consumed my spirit and swallowed me whole

"Wuppin pa nub en all da wong places"
Kept me skinnin' and grinnin' in all the wrong faces
They said I was sexy just so they could sex me
Always hoping that THIS time
I'd be able to look back at THAT moment and say
"THIS is the one that never left me"
But as each one walked, they'd carry a piece of me
along
Til my body grew weaker and my spirit was gone

"She" desperately wants "Me" to tell her that I love
her
But how can I say to this to her when love is
something that I've NEVER felt that for her
"She" made "Me" miserable because she
REFUSED to be
What "My" convoluted perception of beauty came
to be
I just wish "She" would go away and leave "Me"
the hell alone
Because actually, it's HER damn fault that I now sit
here alone
With nobody to tell me

How beautiful I am
How sexy I am

SPILLIN DA PHIYAH

How intelligent I am
How worthy I am
How awesome I am
What a great mom I am
What a wonderful person I am
How deserving I am
Of love

And then "She" caresses "her" skin and wipes away
her tears
And whispers so softly and lovingly in her ear
So quietly she speaks, yet the power of her words
rip the atmosphere

You are beautiful
You are sexy
You are intelligent
You are worthy
You are awesome
You are a great mom
You are a wonderful person
You are so deserving
Of love
And that's why I'll always love you
Now….do you believe "Me" when I say these
things to you?"

And as fresh tears begin to phlow,
"She" smiles through her tears and says,
"Yes, as a matter of fact, I do"

April 3, 2014

EDITED VERSIONS OF MY SOUL

SHE ONLY FELL IN LOVE WITH YOU
To All My Fathers

You wonder what she sees in him
Her once beautiful light is now faded and dim
She's given up so much of herself for him
That the chances of HER returning are growing slim

Used to smile so big it would stretch ear-to-ear
Inward beauty that radiated out....people had to stop
and stare
Saying to themselves, "Now that sista right there
Can make a blind man wanna see and a deaf man
wanna hear"

With a bounce in her step and a sway in her stride
"That's my baby girl!" And you said it with pride
But when that fool took over, it's like something in
her died
And you haven't been able to bring her back to life
no matter how hard you've tried

He tells her to jump...she's already in the air
Make a move without him? She bet not even dare
Self-esteem faded but what does he care
He's the "Head Nigga In Charge" and she's stuck in
his lair

No respect for her feelings, he constantly makes her
cry
The truth ain't never in him, he finds it easier to lie
She continues to wallow in his mess and you don't
understand why
Now you plottin' on 6 million ways for him to die

SPILLIN DA PHIYAH

This is your baby girl and no matter what you gotta
do
You're gonna rescue her from the hell he's putting
her through
But what's rather ironic is that you don't even have a
clue
That some fathers out there are trying to save their
baby girls from you too

August 23, 2015

EDITED VERSIONS OF MY SOUL

SPACE AND OPPORTUNITY

A year and 9 months
Approximately 88 weeks of willing myself
To love you
638 days of trying my damndest to be excited about
Our ongoing union
Roughly 15,341 hours of seeing how well you seem
to interact with others
And wondering why you and I never shared that
same camaraderie
920,070 minutes of believing that today will
FINALLY be THE DAY
That I see you in a far different light and actually
WANT to be with you
402,359, 400 seconds sounds like A LOT of time to
spend
Working on a relationship that I'd already mentally
checked out of
See, as the days went by
I stayed because I thought I had to
As the hours dragged on
I stayed because I felt I needed to
As the seconds ticked away
I stayed because, by then, I was already used to you
And I already knew what to expect when it came to
you
And I didn't want to have to start over again
But the thing is
I really did want to walk away from you
I talked about leaving you THOUSANDS of times
And Lord KNOWS everything in me was ready to
bounce

SPILLIN DA PHIYAH

But still I remained
Telling myself that I didn't want to "jump ship"
until
My back-up plans
Had back-up plans
But apparently you saw right through me
No matter how much I tried to show my love for
you
By simply "showing up" as was expected of me
The mistakes I continued to make served as proof
That my heart no longer belonged to you
So you released me back into the world
I cried tears of shock….but not in front of you
I couldn't let you see the sadness I felt for what
Could've been
I felt….ashamed
Embarrassed even
That you would have the nerve to put ME out
When it should've been I who walked out on
YOU
Yet…at the same time…I felt an inexplicable peace
Dare I say…I was relieved
I know I could've put forth a far greater effort to do
better
And work harder
But I just didn't want to do better
Or work harder
At least….not with you
So thank you for setting me free
You've graciously gifted me the space I need
To pursue the opportunities I want….
My own
402,359, 400 seconds is A LOT of time to spend
Working on a relationship that the mind has already
Checked out of
And I'll never waste THAT kind of time

EDITED VERSIONS OF MY SOUL

Again

May 6, 2014

SPILLIN DA PHIYAH

THE WIFE WINS

You've always been my gurl
A true and constant friend
We're so close we're like sisters
And so we'll be til the very end

But what kinda sista/friend would I be
If I didn't keep it real with you
You see as much as I LOVE you with all my heart
I really don't LIKE some of the things that you do

You're beautiful and smart with such a kind heart
So I truly can't understand
What it is inside of you that makes you think
It's ok to mess with a married man

Now I already know what you're gonna say
"He's the married one, so it's more his fault"
Of course it goes without saying that he's more than
wrong
But as your friend, I'm putting the ball back in
YOUR court

I understand completely that he approached you
first
And he's grimy as all hell for that
But just because he keeps pushing up on you
Doesn't mean that you have to push back

You've seen all his pictures of his wife and kids
His FAMILY --- who he's already told you he'll
NEVER leave
But in the very next breath, because he professes his
love for you

EDITED VERSIONS OF MY SOUL

THAT'S the part you choose to receive

Yeah he tosses a few dollars your way
Pays a couple of bills here-and-there
He even keeps your gas light from coming on
So you think all that proves he cares

You're quickly becoming "that chick"
The same one we used to talk trash about
Calling his phone at all times of the night
Trying hard to disrupt his house

And then you're up here getting mad at HER
Wondering how she could be so stupid to stay
Funny....I often wonder the same thing about you
Especially when to him, you're just a "convenient
lay"

You're constantly breaking plans with your friends
And you keep pushing your family to the side
Just so you can be available IF he calls
And WHEN he doesn't, it's US who comforts your
cries

Where do you spend all your holidays
Most certainly not with him
Oh wait....he MIGHT call you after the festivities
are over
And by then, it ain't the tree he wants to trim

You accuse me of being jealous
Saying I just want what you've got
Riiiiggght.....I wanna be sleeping with a married
man
Who'll never leave his wife and kids for
me.....NOT

SPILLIN DA PHIYAH

I'm really truly tired of watching you
Subject yourself to all this mess
Because as long as you choose to remain in it
Your life will never be blessed

So rest assured I'll ALWAYS fight for you
Of that, you can guarantee
But in the end, I'm going to side with the wife
Because one day, "the wife" could be you or me

Written: December 2013
Revised: November 2015

OUR LIVES MATTER

SPILLIN DA PHIYAH

A DIFFERENT SIMILARITY

BLACK LIVES MATTER!

NO JUSTICE NO PEACE!

BLACK LIVES MATTER!

NO JUSTICE NO PEACE!

NO JUSTICE NO PEACE!

NO JUSTICE NO PEACE!

Man get up outta here with that foolishness

please....

So what so what's the scenario?

Same tragedy....different outcome

So here we go....

Black person

Senselessly killed by White

Outcry public

EDITED VERSIONS OF MY SOUL

It's time to fight

Throw on your battle armor

Cuz we going to war

We ain't taking this lying down

We came to settle the score

We done called in Al Sharpton

Got the NAACP on deck

And we gon' march and we gon' rally

Til we gain back our respect

T-shirts and picket signs

And media coverage on swole

Our voices are being heard

We're accomplishing our goal

Got the WHOLE world chanting

SPILLIN DA PHIYAH

And believing we matter

But when the color scheme changes

Does it become mere chatter?

Black person

Senselessly killed by our own

No public outcry....we just cry out

In the privacy of our homes

"This battle ain't ours

It's the Lord's" we say

Then we "smdh" on Facebook

And charge each other to pray

Yo Al....where you at??

NAACP....what y'all gon' do??

Remember? BLACK LIVES MATTER!

Or is that mantra no longer true?

EDITED VERSIONS OF MY SOUL

Where are the T-shirts and picket signs now?

Media coverage now reduced to a minute

All that passionate venom we just spit last week

What's changed that it's so suddenly diminished?

There is no difference

The blood spilled is all the same

Whether a white person is the perpetrator

Or one of US happens to be the blame

Now when it's "them" against "us" we should

absolutely raise hell

But when it's "us" against "us" the hell-raising

should be worse

We should NEVER be the reason that the last time

A mother lays eyes on her child is in the back of a

hearse

SPILLIN DA PHIYAH

And isn't it a shame that we've become so

desensitized

That violence at OUR hands is no longer tragic

I guess we're hoping that if we ignore it just long

enough

It'll finally disappear into thin air, much like

m.....a........g..........i...............

July 30, 2015

EDITED VERSIONS OF MY SOUL

BACK TO NORMAL
Dedicated to the Emanuel 9

How could something as "normal"

As coming together for prayer

Or welcoming in an outsider

To show him that you genuinely care

Transition into a tragedy such as this

One of epic proportions

My rose-colored glasses are now tainted and gray

My vision....horrifically distorted

I know we shouldn't question You, God

And even in THIS, You get all the glory

But "normal" says 9 people should've returned

home that night

SPILLIN DA PHIYAH

Instead of becoming yet one more heartbreaking

story

Everybody's definition of "normal" is different

As we continue on our merry little way

Doing all those things that are consistent with us

Having just another regular ol' day

But should we be comfortable with getting back to

"doing us"

When someone else's "normal" has been so horribly

disrupted?

The logic that we give...."well life goes on"

In situations like THIS, sounds coldly corrupted

But life DOES go on and soon

Yesterday's happy memories will replace today's

sadness and pain

But let's be real here....no matter how much time

EDITED VERSIONS OF MY SOUL

passes

Nobody's "normal" will ever be normal again

                                        June 25, 2015

SPILLIN DA PHIYAH

BE RIGHT BACK
Dedicated to the Emanuel 9

You said you'd be right back

And I believed you

Said you were running around the corner

Going up the street

Headed down the block

I'm not too sure

I wasn't really listening

I was too pre-occupied with

Preparing dinner

Straightening up the living room

Helping the kids with homework

Just busy being busy

But I promised to put "busy" away as soon as you

got back home

Thing is

You lied to me

EDITED VERSIONS OF MY SOUL

Because you didn't come right back like you said

you would

I sat here waiting

And waiting

And waiting

For you to return

Growing more pissed off by the minute

Blowing up your phone

Hailing barrages of texts at you

All to no avail

Because you never responded

Anger

Turns into hurt

Which quickly becomes

Fear

Where the hell are you

I flop down angrily on the couch and begin flipping

through the channels at the speed of light

SPILLIN DA PHIYAH

Real Housewives of Some Foolishness

Click

Yet another singing talent show

Click

Court show

Click

Basketball

Click

Church shooting

Pause

Downtown

Pause

Emanuel

Pause

9 dead

Quiet

My phone rings suddenly and I begin to breathe

again because finally

EDITED VERSIONS OF MY SOUL

It's you

But it's not you

It's a voice

Telling me I need to come

Downtown

Pause

Something about a

Church shooting

Pause

At

Emanuel

Pause

9 Dead

Quiet

I ask the voice what would be my purpose for

coming down there

See you said you were

Running around the corner

SPILLIN DA PHIYAH

Or going up the street

Or headed down the block

I'm not 100% sure

Because I wasn't really listening

But I distinctly remember you said....

No

YOU PROMISED

That you'd be RIGHT BACK

So again I ask the voice

Why should I come down there

And the voice said

Church shooting

Pause

9 Dead

Pause

Your name

Quiet

And as my world and everything in it slowly began

EDITED VERSIONS OF MY SOUL

to fade to black

All I could think was

Why did you lie to me?

June 22, 2015

SPILLIN DA PHIYAH

BLACKULATION

So my son and 2 of his friends had the GALL

To be walking to another friend's house the other

day

And a cop decided they warranted being stopped

As they journeyed along the way

Were they being obnoxious? Slap-boxing each

other?

Perhaps they were making too much noise?

Were they behaving like animals, running wild in

the streets?

Or were they acting like normal teenage boys?

It truly doesn't matter what the reason is

Because they've all been out shadowed by ONE fact

That the ONLY thing he noticed as he rolled up on

EDITED VERSIONS OF MY SOUL

these boys

Is the color of their skin....BLACK

WWB...Walking While Black

Must really be a legitimate crime

And as that cop approached my son and his friends

I can't help but wonder what was really on his mind

Flashing them with his brights, getting out of his car

And shining his flashlight in each face

And no, says my son, he never patted them down

It doesn't matter though...he'd already violated their

space

I'm STILL choking on a plethora of emotions

From hurt to utter disgust

Because the ones we were taught to call on for

protection

SPILLIN DA PHIYAH

Has now lost EVERY BIT of my trust

Thank God my son tells me that instead of the cop

continuing to harass them

He finally leaves them alone

And all I could do is lift my hands in praise

Because THEY were able come home

And THAT is why we must continue to fight

As we pray and give God all the glory

Our children SHALL be the exception

Rather than the next CNN story

December 19, 2014

EDITED VERSIONS OF MY SOUL

CAN SOMEBODY PLEASE TELL ME WHAT I

DID THOUGH?

God is great!

And God is good!

It's such a beautiful day

In my neighborhood!

I just got paid

And I'm feeling fine;

And running a few errands

Is all that's on my mind.

The first thing I do

Is hit the grocery store.

I pay for my items

And as I'm walkin' out the door,

SPILLIN DA PHIYAH

The alarm goes off

And quicker than a sneeze,

Security swarms like bees,

And brings me to my knees.

I'm confused and disoriented

Because it all happened so fast;

They're going through my bags

And counting my cash;

Vehemently searching

For that imaginary "thing" I took;

I side-eye the cashier,

Throwing her a "help me" look.

She ignores my silent plea

And stares through me instead.

And at that moment I truly wish

EDITED VERSIONS OF MY SOUL

That I hadn't gotten outta bed.

Now here come the cops;

Them "good ol boys in blue;"

Waving their batons;

Hounding me for the "truth."

But I may as well be speaking a foreign language

Because they hear nothing I say.

So I take a deep breath

And quietly I pray.

And then I figure, "HEY!

I'll just show them my receipt!"

So I dig in my pocket

And in a split heartbeat,

What sounds like a million fireworks

SPILLIN DA PHIYAH

Rips through the air;

I see people running;

I hear screaming;

Wait…what just happened here?

Then suddenly a sharp pain cripples me;

I fall flat on my back;

And as I stare up at the ceiling,

Everything starts going black.

I don't even understand…what did I do wrong?

I only came in for 10 items or less.

So can somebody be kind enough to explain to me

How I ended up with 10 holes in my chest?

**From Emmett to Trayvon, to Jordan, Eric and

now Michael; from my baby to your baby, and her

EDITED VERSIONS OF MY SOUL

baby and his baby; ENOUGH really IS ENOUGH!

LEAVE OUR MEN AND BOYS ALONE!!!**

#unarmedyetstillconsidereddangerous

August 12, 2014

SPILLIN DA PHIYAH

COLOR SCHEME

The whites of your eyes

Show the eagerness of your

Black baton

To connect with my brown skin

Your silver badges

Got you fooled into thinking

You have the right to

Make me shed crimson stained tears

But I see how yellow you really are

Your blue uniforms don't hide your

"Green-eyed monster" very well

This fire emanating from my pores

Baffles you

EDITED VERSIONS OF MY SOUL

You see, for reasons far beyond your scope of

understanding

No matter how deep into the ground you may try to

beat us down

We will still rise from the ashes like a Phoenix

The whites of your eyes

Continue to show your disdain

For my brown skin

But at the end of the day

You and I both bleed exactly the same

April 2015

SPILLIN DA PHIYAH

PRAYER OF MARTIN
        ***MARTIN LUTHER KING DAY
                OBSERVANCE***

Gotta get up early

Gotta beat the sun

Too many things to plan and achieve

Before this day is done

I didn't ask for this responsibility

But Lord I put all my trust in You

Because I know You wouldn't have gifted me with

this task

If You weren't going to see me through

So many people are counting on me

To right so many of this country's wrongs

The world is watching me

Please help me to stay strong

EDITED VERSIONS OF MY SOUL

Crosses burning; dogs attacking

Water sprays like bullets in each face

No more rest for the weary

But how much more can we really take

Lord I know You'll never put more on us

Than You already know we could stand

So for every time they try to make us sit down

We need Your help to continue to stand

They want us to bend; they want us to break

Throw our cards on the table and fold

But freedom is right here in our grasp

We MUST reach out and grab hold

That means we'll fight

That means we'll pray

We won't back down

SPILLIN DA PHIYAH

Right here we'll stay

Both day and night

Both night and day

Backing down NOW?

Too huge a price to pay

Future generations are counting on us

So we've GOT to settle this score

This battle is far from over

So for now, we continue this war

January 18, 2015

EDITED VERSIONS OF MY SOUL

YOU STAND CORRECTED

Contrary to "popular" belief

I am not a gangsta nor am I a thug

No, I don't pimp "hos"

And no, surprisingly, I don't sell drugs

I'm not wildin' in these streets

Or trying to pick fights

And I'm always in the house

Before they hit the street lights

No need to clutch your pocketbook

Or cross to the other side of the street

I'm not rocking $200 sneakers

On my feet

I don't sag my pants

SPILLIN DA PHIYAH

And my shirts don't hang to my knees

And I was raised to say

"Yes ma'am"; "No sir"

"Thank you" and "Please"

Despite what you may THINK

I don't wanna impregnate your daughter

My guns will never kill you

They'll just soak you with water

I play basketball and football

And drums in the band

And for the most part, I think

I'm a pretty decent young man

Of course you wouldn't know that

Thanks to your pre-conceived notions

Getting caught up in all the foolishness

EDITED VERSIONS OF MY SOUL

And your ignorant emotions

You judge me

Without even knowing my name

And at the end of the day

My "poor" black skin is to blame

Regardless of your prejudices

I deserve to walk free

Without being afraid of what

You might do to me

And now that you know what I'm really about

I hope now you'll leave me alone

Because contrary to your "popular" belief

I'm just a boy whose mother wants him to come

home

April 16, 2015

I'M STILL HERE

EDITED VERSIONS OF MY SOUL

CASKET READY

Would you think I was suicidal

If I told you I'd rather be dead

I figure being stretched out in a beautiful casket

Is way more comfortable than sleeping on a

"cement bed"

Eyes permanently shut to a judgmental world

That regards me with disgust and disdain

I could escape with the dignity I have left

And close the lid to block out this pain

You're trying to figure out what I did to get here

Assuming it's got to be drugs, or maybe I'm a whore

Seeing nothing but this outer shell of myself

Not realizing I'm still so much more

SPILLIN DA PHIYAH

Than this matted hair

This tired face

This growling stomach

Yearning for just a mere taste

Of the rest of that sandwich

You just threw in the trash

Cuz they forgot the pickles???

Could you BE more crass??

Pay no attention

To these filthy clothes

Or the dirt starting to form

Between my toes

Fingernails chipped

From fluffing my concrete pillow

Fantasizing about the dream home

I'll someday find on Zillow

What IS that smell??

Oh right....it's me

EDITED VERSIONS OF MY SOUL

Rocking my new parfum

Eau du Stale Pee

Haven't washed in months

Man...it'd be so dope

If I could remember what it means

To have water and soap

Tired of praying

Tired of believing

That God hears my prayers

Yet I'm still not receiving

Tired of begging

Tired of crying

Tired of sleeping and waking up

Instead of dying

Tired of hoping

That you'll see me as more

No I'm not strung out on drugs

SPILLIN DA PHIYAH

And no I'm not a whore

But shame on me

For being down on my luck

As the world keeps turnin'

And I remain stuck

Not quite suicidal

But how I wish I was dead

Sleeping in the comfort of my casket

Instead of this cement bed

But since I'm invisible to you anyway

I'm sure you heard nothing I just said....

September 9, 2015

EDITED VERSIONS OF MY SOUL

FOR THE LAST TIME

For every punch to my gut

For every blow to my head

For every stomping of my spirit

For all the tears that I've shed

For every whispered phone call

As I listened out for your voice

For every day that I stayed

Because I didn't think I had a choice

For each and every time

You called me out of my name

For every problem that belonged to you

Yet on my shoulders, you placed all blame

For every time I called the cops

SPILLIN DA PHIYAH

Because "THIS TIME" I've had enough

And for every time I changed my mind

Cuz I couldn't stand to see you handcuffed

For every promise of "Baby, never again"

That quickly turned into multiple lies

For every "Daddy didn't mean to" I told my children

In a feeble attempt to silence their cries

For every story I'd tell about my latest act of

clumsiness

Whenever my friends would question a new bruise

And for every time I'd curse them when they called

my bluff

Because they knew every word was just a ruse

For every "NO"

For every "OUCH"

EDITED VERSIONS OF MY SOUL

For every beating from the bedroom

To the living room couch

For every "STOP"

For every "PLEASE"

For every time, my throat

You'd squeeze

For every time

I'd wish for death

Praying that THIS

Would be my final breath

And yet for some reason

God kept me alive

Which means I have a purpose

And a reason to survive

SPILLIN DA PHIYAH

Physical, mental, verbal

Really....what's in a name?

Emotional, even financial

Abuse is all the same

And while love does bring challenges

It should never bring THAT kind of hurt

So it's time to remember who I was

Before I forgot what I was worth

Time to regain my strength

Time to swallow all fear

Time to take back my life

And finally walk away from here

For every time you said

Nobody else will ever love me

Allow me to introduce you to the new the love in

my life

Me....

October 1, 2015

**To all victims of domestic violence,

past and present, your cries

matter**

SPILLIN DA PHIYAH

HOME SWEET HOME

I knew this day was coming

I've known for a couple months now

But I thought I'd be able to make a way

Even though I had no clue how

I begged and pleaded for another chance

All I needed was a little more time

But apparently my cries fell on plugged-up ears

Because here I am at the finish line

However, this is far from a victory lap

In fact, I don't know how to feel

Disbelief that this is really happening

This moment just seems too unreal

Everything has been packed away in boxes

EDITED VERSIONS OF MY SOUL

Ready to go into storage

And oh how I wish I could unpack some faith

With a heaping amount of courage

Lord why are You allowing this to happen

Am I being punished? Did I do something wrong?

I've been trying my best to do my best

But it seems like I've been struggling for so long

And now the struggle is REALLY real

As I lock and close the door

The realization has painfully hit me

This ain't my home no more

And now here I am in this disgusting building

Confused tears streaming down my face

How many times in the past have I passed by here

And now I'M having to share a space

SPILLIN DA PHIYAH

With all these families I've never seen before

Their stories I don't know

And because there are rules I now have to ask

For permission just to come and go

Belongings shoved in a cubby

And sleeping on a cot

And having to keep a close eye

On everything I've got

100 different personalities

All smooshed into one open space

Sadly, I'm no longer an individual

I am now nothing more than a case

Part of a stack of papers

Strewn all over on someone's desk

Who's overworked and underpaid

EDITED VERSIONS OF MY SOUL

And could probably care less

About any part of my back story

Or what landed me in this position

They don't ask what they can do

To help me out of my situation

They don't ask me about anything

That's doing back flips around in my head

About how I feel like a failure as a mother

Or my impending feelings of dread

I feel like 100 different variations of hell

Certainly disgusted and more than ashamed

I'm the one that put us in this predicament

And I take the full blame

Although my dinky apartment most certainly wasn't

SPILLIN DA PHIYAH

much

At least I could call it my own

But until I can find a job and save up some money

I guess this shelter is now "Home Sweet Home"

Written: November 2013
Revised: November 2015

EDITED VERSIONS OF MY SOUL

I THOUGHT YOU WERE DEAD

I didn't think you'd ever return
Not even sure why you're here
Bombarding my mind
Clouding my thoughts
Wanting me to shed tears again
Making me return to my 12 year old self
Beating myself down

Knowing I caused "this" to happen
"You're so stupid!"
"Why'd you even open the door dummy?"
"You shouldn't have let him hug you!"
"You asked for that!"

You stole my voice
I couldn't tell my mother
Or even my aunt....who I ALWAYS told
EVERYTHING to
My grandmother had just died
They were already sad
You told me if I told them
I'd make them sadder

What I feel in my heart
Has a horrible habit of taking up residence
On my face

My mouth said "Fine" when mommy asked how I
was
My face said....
"Why?? Can you tell he was here?"
"Do you smell his breath on me? He kissed my
neck..."

SPILLIN DA PHIYAH

"Do my shorts still show remnants of his greasy
handprint? He squeezed my bottom..."

You said my grandmother was a wonderful woman
As you kissed my neck
And squeezed my bottom
And at that moment
I hated my body

I hated my over developed breasts
I hated my over developed bottom
I hated this 21 year old's body
Trying to masquerade as a 12 year old's

My body confused you
Made you take unjust advantage of your
"Friend of the Family" status
And when my mother told me years later that you
had passed away
A shrug and an "oh yeah?" was my only reply
Little did she know
You died years ago
At least to me anyway

See, the day I opened the door for you

The same day you hugged me too hard

Which is the same day you hugged me too long

Also the same day you kissed my neck

And squeezed my bottom

All while telling me my grandmother was a
wonderful woman

EDITED VERSIONS OF MY SOUL

I killed you
And buried you
And banished you straight to hell
You've died 1000 deaths over the years
Yet here you are....alive and well

Well no Mr. So-and-So
You may have molested my innocence yesterday
But I will NOT allow you to continue to molest my
spirit today
I didn't think you'd ever return
Not even sure why you're here
But the 41 year old me
Just presented my 12 year old self
With the bestest gift she could ever ask for.....
Her voice

April 20, 2015

SPILLIN DA PHIYAH

SAVE ME
(A Villanelle Poem)

I need to get up....but it's easier to stay asleep
So much on my mind....don't wanna think today
I'm far from depressed....but I'm drowning in the
deep

Harder and faster....tears threaten to creep
"Darkness, please swallow the sun," I pray
I need to get up....but it's easier to stay asleep

Into my bones pain and sorrow do seep
Wrapped in my covers is where I'd much rather stay
I'm far from depressed....but I'm drowning in the
deep

Quiet...please consume me...don't utter ne'er a peep
Choking on my words...I've nothing to say
I need to get up....but it's easier to stay asleep

No longer feeling strong...my soul begins to weep
A million pennies for a mere paltry of peace I would
pay
I'm far from depressed....but I'm drowning in the
deep

Clutching my final fragment of faith, I leap
Finally releasing my worries and allowing Him to
have His way
I need to get up...I will not surrender to sleep
I'm far from depressed...no longer drowning in the

EDITED VERSIONS OF MY SOUL

deep

December 17, 2014

SPILLIN DA PHIYAH

THE GRASS AIN'T ALWAYS GREENER

My man bought me yet another gift today....
A $200 pair of Donna Karans.
You know...the sunglasses?
Yeah...he does that sometimes.
Actually he does that A LOT.
Just buys me expensive gifts out the clear, blue sky.
My girlfriends...I see the slight twinge of green
undertones protruding from their pores.
They see me in yet ANOTHER new exclusively
designed dress;
Stomping the pavement in yet ANOTHER new pair
of Red Bottoms;
Rocking yet ANOTHER new piece of ice in my
ears;
On my wrists;
Around my neck.
Never a hair out of place.
Makeup always beat to perfection.
They tell me they wish their men were like mine...
And all I do is smile and shrug off the ignorance of
their covetousness.
You see,
They don't know that the exclusive designer dresses
perfectly mask the exclusive designer bruises that
cover my back.
They don't know that the Red Bottoms hide the red
bottoms of my feet....as I was made to stand in a tub
of crushed glass for an hour as penance for his
SUSPICION of my cheating.
They have no clue that the ice that covers my ears,
wrists, fingers and neck are nothing more than a
mere upgrade from the ice that I use to cool his
crushing blows.

EDITED VERSIONS OF MY SOUL

If they only knew what I went through on the daily,
they would know that I only rock the best weaves
that money can buy to hide the obvious patches
where my natural hair has been ripped from my
scalp.
My makeup stays "beat" to hide each and every
beating he lays upon my face.
Yes it's true...
I got more clothes
And shoes
And jewelry
And purses
And weave
And crap than you can swing a stick at.
But instead of me packing up and leaving, clothed
in nothing but the last shred of dignity I have left,
I continue to suck it up, keep smiling at my
girlfriends' envy and anticipate the next swing of the
stick,
And the goodies it'll get me.

Originally Titled: DONNA KARAN
Written: January 18, 1999
Revised: September 12, 2014

WRITE ON SISTA

EDITED VERSIONS OF MY SOUL

BIRTHWRITE

This is the poem that Jayne wrote

These are the words
That birthed the poem
That Jayne wrote

This the ink
That spilled the words
That birthed the poem
That Jayne wrote

This the pen
That spit the ink
That spilled the words
That birthed the poem
That Jayne wrote

These are the fingertips, calloused and sore
That gripped the pen
That spit the ink
That spilled the words
That birthed the poem
That Jayne wrote

This is the fire, heat seeping from every pore
That burned the fingertips, calloused and sore
That gripped the pen
That spit the ink
That spilled the words
That birthed the poem
That Jayne wrote

These are the thoughts, daring me to explore

SPILLIN DA PHIYAH

That ignited the fire, heat seeping from every pore
That burned the fingertips, calloused and sore
That gripped the pen
That spit the ink
That spilled the words
That birthed the poem
That Jayne wrote

These are the memories, kicking open my mind's
door
That produced the thoughts, daring me to explore
That ignited the fire, heat seeping from every pore
That burned the fingertips, calloused and sore
That gripped the pen
That spit the ink
That spilled the words
That birthed the poem
That Jayne wrote

This is pure love and pain, consistently at war
That summon the memories, kicking open my
mind's door
That produced the thoughts, daring me to explore
That ignited the fire, heat seeping from every pore
That burned the fingertips, calloused and sore
That gripped the pen
That spit the ink
That spilled the words
That birthed the poem
That Jayne wrote

This is my passion, I'll submit forever more
This is pure love and pain, consistently at war
That summoned the memories, kicking open my
mind's door
That produced the thoughts, daring me to explore

That ignited the fire, heat seeping from every pore
That burned the fingertips, calloused and sore
That gripped the pen
That spit the ink
That spilled the words
That birthed the poem
That Jayne wrote

September 22, 2015

***In the style of the nursery rhyme "The
House That Jack Built" by Mother
Goose***

SPILLIN DA PHIYAH

I WRITE BECAUSE....

I write because nobody listens
I spill my ink over pipe dreams and wishes
Praying for strength as my tears start to fall
Lord help me reach the masses or no one at all
Hand them my heart with a bow wrapped around it
Used to not have a voice but thanks to Poetry, I
found it
I refuse to be silenced, I got TOO much to say
No longer caring who's listening cuz I'mma spit
anyway
And with my fist clenching my pen, I raise it high in
the air
Whatchu wanna hear today folks?
Truth or dare?

I write because nobody listens
And because God didn't allow it to kill my vision
Words slice through my heart like a lyrical incision
Ink fires like bullets hitting the page like
ammunition
Bringing every thought that I've wrought to fruition
Releasing this poetic beast is my soul's only
mission
Spittin' whatever the hell I feel, never seeking
permission
Each write is orgasmic, a well-versed emission
Tongue-lashing every ear with diabolical precision
Now look what you miss when you don't pay
attention....

January 26, 2015

EDITED VERSIONS OF MY SOUL

POETRY IS…

Poetry is…

What it's always been
My late-night lover
My all-day friend
My hand-holder when I feel alone
On this massive earth
The seed I've nursed since birth
Poetry showed me my worth
They're the words that God
Has chosen me to release
In the midst of raging storms
Poetry is my peace

It turns me on
It turns me out
It transitioned my diminutive voice
Into a shout
It makes me believe
I'm able to receive
It allows me to laugh
It allows me to grieve
It's my 100 watt bulb
In the darkest of night
It gives me the strength
To continue my fight
These sheets become my boxing ring
This pen…my gloves
And no matter how severe the blood "Phlows"
It's STILL love

SPILLIN DA PHIYAH

Poetry is you
Poetry is me
Poetry is us
Poetry is we
Poetry is our truth
And it will always be free
Poetry is my permission
To be....

October 26, 2014

EDITED VERSIONS OF MY SOUL

POETRY SAID I COULD

You stepped to me at time when my voice
Was non-existent
Unsure of the woman I was becoming
Afraid to trouble the waters
Because of the impending storms ahead
No need to speak
The people I wanted to hear me
Weren't listening anyway

But you got me blossoming
Uprooting my words like flowers from fresh soil
Never judging what I say
Or how I choose to say it
You told me I have the right to speak
Whether it be from my heart
Or from the very pits of my soul
You told me I have the right to speak

Whether it be about love's blissful beginnings
Or the putrid stench of its bitter demise
From joy to pain
From sunshine to rain
From happy to sad
From good to bad
From perfectly pissed to disgustingly dissed
From dawn's early light to my first and last kiss

One line
Two lines
Three lines
Four
You gave me back to me
Plus so much more

SPILLIN DA PHIYAH

My confidence
My strength
My peace
My heart
My voice

This voice that has the audacity to believe that it
Shouldn't be silenced
After all
It was YOU who told me I have the right to speak
So out of ANY pen
Onto ANY page
Into ANY mic
Standing firmly on ANY stage

Speak?   Alright now....you asked for it! ;-)

July 14, 2014

EDITED VERSIONS OF MY SOUL

THAT WOMAN

I am the air that you breathe
I am the spark in your flame
I am the one whose mere presence
Eases everyone's pain
I am always getting better
I am souls coming together
I am the denim in these jeans
I am the cotton in this sweater
I am THAT WOMAN
Nothing more, nothing less
And that's all the proof you need that
I AM THE BEST
That's right I am always
Able and willing
I deserve top billing
Some people may classify me as crazy
And I admit my ideas are sometimes hazy
But once you see the end result
Nicely laid out on a platter
The presentation is so fly
The "crazy" no longer matters
I stay on my climb
All day and every night
And with God on my side
Everything is already alright
I am a "never-ending story"
I am the cat's meow
I am the who, what and when
The where, why and how
I am THAT WOMAN
Nothing more, nothing less
So just call me "Johnny" cuz I stay on a "Quest"
Yes! I am poise and I am grace

SPILLIN DA PHIYAH

I am flannel and I am lace
No my name is definitely NOT baby
So when you see me "PHLOW'in" through these
streets
I expect to be approached as a lady
My mind is always clicking and whirring
It never, ever stops
And I may not have very much
But what I have sho nuff's a lot
I am that "awwww sooky-sooky now"
I am that "oooh lawd ha'mercy now"
I know you thought I couldn't but as you can clearly
see, I can
I am much more woman than most people can stand
I apologize if I sound cocky
And I'm certainly not trying to sound mean
But I really am the coolest thing walking
I see me as a QUEEN
Just the sound of my voice has made men's knees
shake
But I no longer have time for games
Because I have far too much at stake
Yes I am every heartbeat
And I am that beautiful music you hear in the streets
I am the left and the right side of your brain
And I'm sure I'm everything that also drives you
insane
I am intelligent conversation
I am that cool, tingly sensation
My personality gets you drunker than liquor
And keeps you ten times higher than weed
I am 10,000% of EVERYTHING that you need
I am some of what you thought I was
And probably most of what you heard
I am the first and the second
The this, that AND the third

EDITED VERSIONS OF MY SOUL

I hope you got plenty of water
Because I constantly and consistently bring the fire
And I'mma keep on doing my thang
Even long after I retire
And how do I know this?
Well I've been saying why this whole time now
It's because I am THAT WOMAN
Nothing more, nothing less
And that's all the proof you need that
I AM THE BEST

Circa: 1995
Revised: January 2014

THIS CHICK HERE
(A Rondel Poem)

So many lines define this body of mine
Roads have been harried...yet I travel on
Giving my all til the day I am gone
Far from perfection....but I'm doing just fine

So many times I've prayed for a sign
Am I doing my best as I journey along?
So many lines define this body of mine
Roads have been harried...yet I travel on

Lost a lot of loves...still I continue to cross that line
Refusing to settle....yet not settling to remain alone
Hoping to one day find this love of my own
No more inhibitions....wouldn't that be divine?

So many lines define this body of mine

December 14, 2014

EDITED VERSIONS OF MY SOUL

TIL HER VERY LAST BREATH

What WAS her name?
Was it Tiffany or Jayne?
Was she loving and supportive?
Or did she constantly lash out in pain?

Did she do everything she could
To be part of the common good?
Did she do things because she WANTED to
And not simply because she SHOULD?

Did she speak life in every ear
Whether or not they chose to hear?
Did she sincerely reciprocate each hug?
Sincerely wiped away each tear?

Was she always as strong as people perceived her to
be?
Never too weak to stare adversity down
Was she always wearing the proper shoes
When it came to stomping Satan to the ground?

She was definitely all woman
That you can believe
One never nervous
To drape her heart 'cross her sleeve

She was your mother
Your daughter
Your sister
Your friend
And you'll always remember these pieces of her

SPILLIN DA PHIYAH

In every piece she allowed to spill from her pen

December 1, 2014

EDITED VERSIONS OF MY SOUL

YOU KNOW YOU LOVE MY HAIR

She's survived ponytails
And afro puffs
Shirley Temple Curls
And barrettes and stuff
Saturday morning hot combs
For Sunday School
That feel of heat on ya "kitchen"
That was never cool
Then came the Jheri Curl
With the Jheri Curl drip
And the "kssshhh kssshhh" sound
Falling from every lip
Don't forget the Salt-n-Pepa
And the T-Boz cut
Oh, and the Patra braids
Hanging down to our butt
Halle Berry had us in
The salon from sun up to down
To make sure our 'do was laid
And turnin' heads around town
From glued tracks to sew-ins
To finger waves to pin curls
From French rolls to pinned-up buns
And all us "au naturale" girls
With our "TWA's"
And our big ass 'fros
From 2-strand twists to dredlocs
Man ANYTHING goes
From cornrows to "Celie" braids
From the 27-Piece to the fresh cold Fade
From 1B/30 to the Brazilian Blowout
Throw on a Lace Front Wig when we want to show
out

SPILLIN DA PHIYAH

From our various textures
To the colors we RAWK
We sistas wear the crowns
That make many mouths drop
So talk all you want about it
But the reason you stop and stare
Is because as much as you hate to admit it
YOU KNOW YOU LOVE MY HAIR

April 14, 2014

NAKED

PREFACE

The final piece in this book is one that I really did not want to write. It is too real; it is too grimy; it is too in your face; but it is my reality. It literally scares the hell out of me every time I see the words laid out in front of me because as I read them, I know that they are true. If you are completely honest with yourself, these words may ring true for you as well. I know that everybody is not ready for THIS kind of realness; this is why I saved this piece for last. If you choose to turn this page, just know that this piece is as hardcore as they come. I have not minced any words, nor have I "cleaned" it up so much that it takes away from the message. If you choose to read, I only ask that you keep an open mind and realize that while this may very not be

YOUR truth, it IS somebody's truth, and after reading this, they now know that they are not alone in their struggle.

~jp~

SPILLIN DA PHIYAH

SPIRITUAL WARFARE

All these spirits up insida me

And nunna these spirits will just let me be

Whispering in my ear and disturbing my sleep

Dredging up feelings I thought I'd buried deep

Spirits of hurt and spirits of pain

Sprits of clouds and spirits of rain

Spirits of teeth and spirits of tongues

Spirits that insist on keeping me sprung

Spirits of fingers dancing up and down my back

Spirits of Jimmy and Johnson and Jack

Spirits of some Toms and some Harrys too

But "D," you the one that keeps me stuck like glue

Spirits got me catching flashbacks at the light

Spirits got me touching myself at night

Feeling all convicted cuz don't the Bible say that's

EDITED VERSIONS OF MY SOUL

wrong

But man I ain't had me no "D" in soooo long

I be tryna ignore all them urges I got

But them spirits just will not shut the hell up

Won't get out my head, won't leave me alone

And the more trash they talk, the more I feel all

alone

All I want is a little bitta "D," is that really such a

bad thing

But if I continue getting random "D," will I possibly

never get a ring

I'm tryin my absolute damndest not to be out here

fornicating

And since I ain't out here running these streets, so

what if I'm masturbating

Master, this is so frustrating! What do You expect

me to do

I'm constantly horny and lustful but I wanna do

right by You

I try real hard to pray real loud and drown them

voices out

But them spirits Lord them spirits just won't get the

hell out

They keep tempting me and teasing me and spitting

da foolishness

Like "well since you ain't got no "D," gone handle

it yo'self"

NO! NO NOOOOOOOO!

Cuz 1 Peter, chap 2, verse 11 says: "Dearly beloved,

I beseech you as strangers and pilgrims, abstain

from fleshly lusts, which war against the soul."

And 1 Thessalonians, chap 4, verse 4 says: "That

everyone of [us] should know how to possess His

vessel in sanctification and honour."

EDITED VERSIONS OF MY SOUL

Oh and let's not forget 1 Corinthians, chap 10, verse 13, which says: "There hath no temptation taken you but such as is common to man; but God is faithful, who will not suffer you to be tempted above that ye are able; but will with the temptation also make a way to escape, that ye may be able to bear it...."

Well then, there you have it.....

See, although "D" is my temptation

That makes me wanna succumb to fornication

Because God really IS faithful

My escape is masturbation....right....?

RIGHT?!

All these spirits still up insida me

SPILLIN DA PHIYAH

Still tempting my flesh, not leaving me be

And I'm weak….and I'm tired

And I just wanna be free….

Written: September 2013
Revised: November 2015

AND THAT'S THAT PIECE...

BACK COVER

Spillin' da Phiyah: Edited Version of My Soul is a combination of pieces selected from Jayne's 2 previous books: Get a Grip: Spilled Ink from My Soul and Phiyah Phlows. Those who are familiar with her previous offerings will recognize that the messages are EXACTLY the same; just minus A LOT of the "additional" language. You can follow Jayne on Facebook (Jayne Phlow); on her Facebook fan page (The Jayne Phlow Experience); on Instagram (@thejaynephlowexperience); and on SoundCloud (Jayne-Phlow).

www.ingramcontent.com/pod-product-compliance
Lightning Source LLC
Chambersburg PA
CBHW031958040426
42448CB00006B/413